Multitudes

Poems and Such

by
Pér Himself

Multitudes

by Pér Flood

Published 2017 by Pér Flood

This book is licensed for your personal enjoyment and education only. While best efforts have been used, the author and publisher are not offering legal, accounting, medical, or any other professional services advice and make no representations or warranties of any kind and assume no liabilities of any kind with respect to the accuracy or completeness of the contents and specifically disclaim any implied warranties of merchantability or fitness of use for a particular purpose, nor shall they be held liable or responsible to any person or entity with respect to any loss or incidental or consequential damages caused, or alleged to have been caused, directly or indirectly, by the information or programs contained herein. Stories, characters, and entities are fictional. Any likeness to actual persons, either living or dead, is strictly coincidental.

All rights reserved. No part of this publication may be reproduced or transmitted in any form or by any means, electronic or mechanical, including photocopying, recording, or by any information storage and retrieval system, without permission in writing from the publisher. All images are free to use or share, even commercially, according to Google at the time of publication unless otherwise noted. Thank you for respecting the hard work of the author(s) and everyone else involved.

Copyright © 2017 Pér Flood

Authors and sources cited throughout retain the copyright to their respective materials.

Table Of Contents

Dedication & Acknowledgements 1
About Pér 3
HOW TO READ THIS BOOK IN TWELVE STEPS: 5
Connect with Me 7
Foreword 9
I constrain Multitudes 13
My heart bursts 15
What if 16
Shroud of Memphis 18
dealing with death 20
in between 22
birds gotta 24
Sunrise 26
Invisible man on base 28
behind the shed 30
I have been drinking 32
easy together 33
Played Pantry 36
Hands 38
wrong again 40
SO BE IT 41
Vegas reflection 43
Circles 44
the snake 45
page one 46

Pure Genius	47
sunset in the alley	48
not the cruelest	49
galaxy 500	50
modern photography	51
Impeccable medicine card	52
Motivationally speaking	54
from the void	56
choices	57
For Elsa	58
moments in the sun	60
postcards from the coast	62
gift of time	64
Crow	67
early sunday morning at Caffe Vita	68
Living out loud	70
so much buckshot	73
in between	74
tenth and yamhill	76
shriek	77
bring in the clowns	78
guns and blood	79
evolution	80
spontaneous pop song	81
less	82
a wing and a prayer	83
518 AM In Tempe	85

heard	86
The Virgin Berth	88
train of skitchin thoughts	89
Fight	92
snow tires	94
Let Us Prey	96
Storm's a comin	98
nashville gloom	100
corn husks and crickets	102
Connect with Me	105
About Pér	107

Dedication & Acknowledgements

For:

Angi
You see the world in such a beautiful way and you choose to share that with me. Thank you for the gift of love, time and belief.

Loretta Jacquelyn Distell Flood AKA Jackie
You always reminded me that I was your favorite child and now it is in print.

Frederick J Cusack
The way you adored Peggy is an inspiration.
The way you adore Angi is phenomenal.
Our friendship is immeasurable.

Special thanks to:

Richard Jefferson White for making me feel like I was good enough to do this and for suggestively editing this work.

Andy Decker for letting me use and abuse your beautiful painting ***Rusty Chainz & Black Eyed Suzie*** for the cover and for inspiring me through your dedication to art and nature.
https://www.facebook.com/AndyDeckerForrealism/
http://www.modusartgallery.net/andy-decker-artist

Jon and Adam Schlegel for dreaming up a little breakfast restaurant that would change people's lives in ways few could imagine and for bringing me along for the ride. You also hired a whole mess of great people who have enriched my life in ways I am still sorting out.

Graphic Designer:
Andy Mason who wrapped a cover around my words
http://www.andythings.com

Thanks to everyone who ever encouraged me and to everyone who reads my words.

About Pér

Pér Himself has lived a multitude of lives, worked a multitude of jobs, and played in countless punk, rockabilly, and hard-to-classify bands. From digging ditches to singing telegrams, Pér has done it all while writing with the passionate heart that beats in all great American poets. Pér observes life from unique angles, bringing a syncopated view of the world around and within to readers in a relatable and often humorous way. Pér finds it funny anyway.

From Pér Himself About Pér Himself

In the fifth grade I wrote "I HATE HATE HATE MYSELF!" in the top margin of a school paper on which I received a bad grade I knew then that I had to be a writer. That is only half true. I did write that, fully unaware that the paper had to be returned to the teacher.. I did not know then that I had to be a writer but I did learn that I had to be a bit more discreet about my self-loathing.

That was then.

Much of my life has not really been lived fully in the moment because I've been mostly thinking about how I am going to write about the moment in a way that will invite someone who was not there to share the moment, to help someone who was there relive the moment, or both. This is a good thing. Once I heard someone laugh or saw them tear up over something I had written I felt a connection like none I had ever known. I hope my writing will connect us in some meaningful way.

If creativity exists it finds its way to the light. One might pour themselves into their work or into their family or just pour themselves another drink until they become an expert at something even if that expertise is in avoiding doing what they love because they are afraid. A love of language whether written spoken or sung has woven it's way into everything I have done as a JOB whether that was rewriting an entire singing telegram routine on the fly, inserting inside jokes into drink menu descriptions or talking a fellow employee off the cliff. The best feeling of all was surprising a guest who was having a rough day by making them smile, remembering their story or giving them a free pancake (God bless Snooze An AM Eatery!).

HOW TO READ THIS BOOK IN TWELVE STEPS:

You could approach this book as I approached writing it which is randomly and over many years or seldom and over many beers.

The 12 Steps program to Get The Most Out of This Book:
1. Grab the book and maybe a cocktail and head outside
2. Open to a random page
3. Read that page and ponder the vast undercurrent of connectivity in our lives
4. Disregard step 3 if you wish
5. Put the punctuation wherever your mind chooses
6. Feel free to judge
7. Feel free to think of this as not poetry
8. Feel free to share your thoughts
9. Feel free to keep your thoughts to yourself
10. Think long hard and loudly about how you could do better than this
11. Do better than this
12. Send me a copy

Connect with Me

Visit me at

www.perhimself.com

or

http://www.Twitter.com/PerHimself

Or
https://www.facebook.com/profile.php?id=100017467620963

Foreword

Pér and I once worked together behind the bar of a frenetic little restaurant in Denver, Colorado. The money was good but the shifts were long, even by service industry standards, and the music chosen by the management was often, to our ears, impossibly lame. The irritation was easy to come by but hard to conceal. I was in my early twenties then, with ambitions of becoming the next literary wunderkind, so of course when faced with such titanic injustices, more often than not, I capsized.

Pér took another approach. Like all good bartenders, he found a way to blend frustration with humor into a kind of veil-dropping honesty that earned him respect. If you were moving too slow, which I often was, or if you ordered a drink from him like he was just another bartender there to do as you wished, he'd let you know it, but with his trademark disarming wit. Being from Arkansas, I most often received from Pér an exaggerated Southern drawl - loud enough to get a laugh from our customers, of course - with discussion of cousins and banjos and bare feet. In so doing, he got me moving faster at the mixing station, but more importantly, he won a reputation with guests for his wit and his humanity. He was good company. Every day he worked, he had many regulars visit the bar just to see him, and with them, even sometimes at their eager expense, Pér always had lots of fun.

So it is with his poetry. All of the usual grievances of the capital-p Poet are present here, of course: religion, politics, childhood, even the great tyranny that is the working world. Within any of these subjects is enough material to drive each of us to our own brand of madness. Pér knows this, we can be sure. But here on the page is that same sharp-witted, big-hearted bartender who slung puns as fast as he slung drinks. He is nothing if not aware of the justification for our collective despondence, but he is unwilling to allow such sorrow to manifest in himself. There is too much beauty in the backyard for that, too much pleasure in playing with the written word. Beware: if there is humor in a homophone, Pér will find it, and thank God. For even in its heaviest moments, Per's is a poetry of joy. He is having fun here. And his gift to us, as it was to his barflies, is levity. That, I suspect, is precisely what turns readers into regulars. I'll drink to that. As Pér likes to say: "Cheers, big ears!"

Richard Harrison White
Wilson, Arkansas
May 14, 2017

Flood / Multitudes / 11

KILU LAVA

I constrain Multitudes

I have created entire universes in a single beam of light
galactic fireflies laying eggs on iridescent teardrops
falling from the eyes of god
knitting snakes like so much
LED yarn through wormholes
to emerge as brilliant glowing screen doors
opening to reveal the milky whiteness
covering andromeda strains
with the thin skin of scaly stars
reflecting
refracting
distracting the armchair detective
the lab coat technician
toward the universal mistruths
evident to the unequal self
constituting an obfuscated conundrum
to patch the evil eye
redirecting shadows
toward the untoward underbelly
from which they emerged
the slimy white bloated underbelly
where they lay eating in their own effluence
cheating their way to influence
Inbreeding their way to affluence
Greed-ing their way to indifference
Insult spewing intolerants
through sleight-of-hand chicanery
whitewashing brains
of those
long circling the drains
of life's cesspools
who amongst us
can sink
this ship of fools

My heart bursts

my eyes feel so wide open today
along with my heart
tugging on my ears
I am so excited to be alive
ready to ride this wave
as long as it rolls
so will I

A butterfly flapped
on the other side of the world
now I have a tsunami
going on up in here
I am noticing things
that I once passed by
and vice versa

This giant space is
just what I need
yet it can barely contain me
The bamboo interior
calms and inspires
the coffee may
as well be rocket fuel

so filled with gratitude
turning over a new
belief system
all juiced up
and ready to dance
to kung fu fighting
like a madman

What if

what if I did all this prep
drove here from there for atmosphere
set up this table just so
ordered the proper fuel
drank that fuel
set up the keyboard
outstretched my digits
and nothing
nothing on the brain
nowhere to begin
nothing to obtain

what if I moved outside?
the AC is chilling my brain stem
shit the chatty women just took it
and I don't want to make a scene
the funnel cloud starts forming
thoughts thrown like cows
around the cornfields of my mind
until they land in a trailer park of ideas
where I open the roofs like lids
on tins of potted meat
so I can suck out the tasty bits

what if The black jacked pickup with the bad ass tires
parked by the curb
belonged to me?
I would be looking at the world through limousine tinted windows bitch
I would laugh at
the pasty faced blonde
who just left the coffee shop
to find a ticket on her windshield
a parking meter with no head
was too good to be true
I would sit judging in my pickup
with the cattle guard on front
I would be all lifted and lofty

what if I ate soft serve for breakfast
every day
until the Guinness book authors tracked me down
what if I got a tattoo of your face on my face
so I could see you in the mirror each day
what if I wrote down all my thoughts
just to scare everyone away
what if my thoughts were really being monitored
by satellites and lizards
conspiracy theorists and special forces

Shroud of Memphis

separated at birth
mama's pretty boy

mixed up shook up
robin hood
stealing from the
rich black culture
feeding to the poor
starving whites

drawing an angelic voice
from its quiver
delivering love arrows
through unintended hearts

in fits and starts
egg beater legs
swing from the devil's hips
stirring a sleepy uptight nation

stereotyped in
film after horrible film
pigeonholed
imitated
never syncopated
diminished
reduced to a lip and a swagger
the king of whiteness
in a camp all his own

possessed by repression
following a leader
who complicated simplicity
neglecting what was perfection
for perception and
a large percent of his persona

Purse strings bulging like an
encrusted jumpsuit

a posse forms to kill a wanted man
with a stew of reds and blues

a pathetic patriotic patriarch
sings god bless america
while bombs fall on a land
of future impersonators

mutton-chops
sunglasses
on stage kung fu
a big man shrouded in
a young man's talent

dealing with death

so how does one deal with death?
one does not deal as all do
because we all have a
voodoo that we each do so well
or don't
or we just do what we know
then we know it differently the next time

some of us pace
some of us pray
some of us find grace
some of us drink the pain away
some of us blame
some of us curse
some burst
into flames
or far worse
ashes to ashes
caskets to urns
knights without sashes
turn turn turn

too few funeral pyres
or burials at sea
oh say can you
burn this vessel
called me?

light me up
dance through my smoke
as you all did in life
pretend you got my joke
I won't make you suffer
as christ did on the cross
just say a few odd words
then dance to "Let's get lost"

If some blasphemer rises
and misbehaves

to say that on my death bed
I decried that Jesus saves
anymore than you can
on a TV or a couch
believe just one percent of
what he says
and don't smoke what's in his pouch

in between

It's 3:13 AM or so
and the cats are on me like hyenas
on fresh kill
the big guy pinning my shoulder
marking my jawline
the little one tucking in behind my knees
to jackknife my legs
they move like long time tag team wrestling partners
I'm so thirsty yet I don't want to disturb them
so aware that the life preserver of sleep
drifted toward the pitch black horizon ten minutes ago
so not wanting to wake her
so not wanting to lose my dreamy genius

I am not cool enough to be an insomniac
I am just old enough to need a bathroom break
around this time
or I am being healthier by drinking enough water
to wake even a younger me
around this time
this time when a younger me would have been passing out
after the show
ears still ringing a bit
Beer already turning to sour morning breath behind my dopey curled smile
close curtain cue the dream cycle prepare hangover

The house is glossy and still ship shape from her return
the order eases my mind
the shiny countertop creates puddles of digital clock mockery
of my sleeplessness
As the cliche train whistle blows though no one would believe me
Heading to parts well mapped
I think now that I did not sleep so much as I napped
I splash cold water on my eyelids
to bring me from the in-between
to the thought hunter gatherer typist mode
we've lost a lot of good words to this state of mind
and dammit I am not about to lose any more

I fret over every sound even the dogs tap dancing claws on the floorboards
So glad now that I oiled the hinges
so glad now that I live in an age of soft computer keyboards
and not woodpecker typewriters with their bells and crumpled paper edits
She wakes in spite of my church mouse morphing
I increase my stealth
she returns to bed without crossing the threshold
She needs her sleep
not for beauty
but to wash away the sins of her unending workload
to slay the dragons of travel and the low slung arrows of petty tyrants
emailing edicts and ultimatums at all times of day and now
Sleepless slitherers hissing and moaning in an effort to make their jobs seem necessary
bringing meaning to the meaningless

just before I awoke
I sat next to a man at the end of a u-shaped bar facing west
he was to my right trying to win the cracker jack game so tiny in his hands
all angles were attempted tongue slung over his lip like Sinatra's jacket
over the shoulder of his tailored shirt
the dude exuding so much frustration upon not winning this un-winnable game
then my dream narrator spoke frankly in my mind's ear saying
and this guy is the head of maintenance at the country's largest nuclear plant?
I think I am glad I awoke before that dream played out
Let's go see what dreams the couch will conjure
she needs her sleep
and so do I

birds gotta

no headphones
allows the birds comments to
penetrate my moribund gin soaked mind
these are new birds or perhaps
old birds singing new songs
songs of spring
songs of good things to come
warbling like a snake charmer's flute
asking worms to the dance
perhaps they are just judging me
as am I
such self importance
like birds have the time
they do seem to be
looking down their beaks
I am unruffled
down the frost bitten street
I continue my shuffle

the songs open my eyes as well as my ears
now I see crocus unraveling
tulips ascending from dormancy
school busses become bumble bees
collecting students like pollen
then buzzing away
here's to hoping we all
learn something new today
the cars are full of drones
heading to the hive
to perform the tasks
they have been programed to perform
again and again
until gold watch
or pink slip

birds sing
because they have to
I listen
because I choose to

I also choose to believe
the birds sing for me

Sunrise

for the love of a sunrise
I would quit my job
declare bankruptcy
lose this thing i have
be alone
cold
and sleepy
there i was
sitting still
while the rising tide
roared by
on radial tires
unaware
and
unencumbered
by my presence
I may as well have been
a speed bump
or a
buffalo
a terrorist
or a
shadow
racing the sun
every
ground
is sacred
every sound
is a
vacant lot
all our slates
are clean
and each rising
of the sun
makes the
sins of the night
before
come undone
but you must pause

and look
with reverence
to the east
to the new life
you have earned

Invisible man on base

Every night I wonder if I am a writer
every morning I wake up early to
ponder my death
so I think that makes me a writer

words coalesce uncooperatively
occupying low rent districts
puddling
like the murky water
in the clay path
behind our growing up house
where we ran and slid
into next week
into puberty
giggling
not worrying about
glass or razor blades
just reveling in the slick mud
tickling
soothing
our childhood spa
was a clay path alley
now a paved street
where life was complete
for us
uncomplicated
dedicated
to running faster
in new Keds
jumping higher
off the shed
no disasters
nine feet off the grass
no one got plastered
Mister Shannon's field was Wrigley field
just across the clay path
slash alleyway

the sky was a blue forever

we were clever
under silver clouds
building backstops
so we could play
four kid baseball
all fields open
invisible men on base
I still remember running hard
from center field
to first
diving to catch
a ball in an acid burned glove
to be immortal
here now in my mind's eye

We were kids
building a stadium
we set up bases
we were four beings
playing a game involving us
and fourteen imaginary players
countless umpires and
go fuck yourselves others
We lived underneath an umbrella of
parental madness
unstoppable oppression
and unlimited imagination
to play our version of baseball
where we were
all the invisible man
on base
when we needed to be

behind the shed

I shed my skin today
While in an acupunctural trance
just after I passed the rat that has been nesting in my chest over my liver
I ejected the rat just like a snake would
muscles moving like a slinky toward my tail
this happened after I felt my heart glow with the golden light of the sun
my chest filling with a warrior's breathe
the last of the skin was pulled from my body by an unknown helper at my feet
tugging away until I lay skinless and pearlescent
like a conglomeration of bright white light citrus cells exposed to the world
next I saw a sandy white landscape surrounding me
I hazily realized this place was the Bonneville Salt Flats
and I have to get there soon
soon like this year
I have never been but looking at pictures
now I see that it is what I saw
down to the pixels
lying there on the table
I need to go lie on the flats
flat on my back
to absorb what I lack
from the outside in
sun cracking my shell
sending the rat back to hell
these events
these visions
were as real as this computer
as real as this sunset
as real as these giant pines surrounding me
protecting me
enlightening me
as real as the endless din
of traffic headed out and in
past the neighborhood palace of skin and
what some would call sin

everything is a byzantine serpentine
maze of life death and regurgitation for me lately
all circles leading back to that viper's fang in my leg
still pulsing
back to the venom in my veins
to the scales I seek to balance
to my clandestine dalliance
with the rattle of death
and the hot breath of
forgiveness

I have been drinking

I have been drinking
and punching at the air
floating away on soft pillows of thought
losing worry and dread
smiling as if I know something you don't
rubbing my face softly
appreciating music more
and louder than usual
wanting to talk story

I'm very sure of my opinions now
looking for someone
who disagrees sharply
so we can debate until one of you
bystanders grows weary
and makes us agree to be at odds
until one can be disproved in the future
and it isn't gonna be me

I'm loving people more now
seeing through my prejudices
and previous pre-determinations
right down to their sweet soft souls
we are all equal here
where one veil comes down
the other comes off altogether
I wonder why we can't
see things this way all the time

no pain
no bad memories
i am here now
and so I'll remember tomorrow
what now feels like
I am writing it down

I have no excuses
I have some regrets
I have no fear

easy together

Just as we were together
alone in Paris
We are alone now
in the mountains
Back at our spot
the place others might shun
our quiet place
closer to the sun
cradled by
well educated mountains
sung to by an icy creek
spoiled by fine food
and warmed by strong spirits
finding comfort in the way
we enjoy each other

Elsa our shrimp tailed dog
helps with housecleaning
a spill here
a drop there
she also gives us reason
to walk farther
during varying degrees
of solar or lunar light
expanding our vision
we are as excited for
sunrise with flapjacks
as we are for
magazine inspired
meat pinwheels
with scalloped potatoes
in a rich sauce Frances

we move without effort
easy like sliding on ice
wordless communication
languid as a breeze
through the pines
her applying a light scent

me asking her to hold still
so I might kiss her hair
completing each others view
from bighorn sheep
to ramshackle motel
from doll-heads on saplings
to Elsa's emotional state
from good morning to
give me back my pillow

Played Pantry

The petite bat-like chihuahua
peeked out of her loose grey t-shirt
resting on the right of her more than ample breasts
which both rested half way out on her even more than ample belly
which fell like play-doh squeezed from a fun factory nozzle over
her designer blue jeans
toward the convenience store floor
I think she was wearing boots
or maybe those were worn by her counterpart
The poor little shivering pup thought about taking a lick
from the woman's more than ample milk shake
the one made on site by a milk shake slurpy-like machine
the woman went on to the clerk about how good they taste
the clerk said we don't have those machines at my usual store
Where's that? Belmont and 30th
the dog knew the milkshake would bring more shivers or worse
turning up it's little button of a nose and I am sure he is not the first
during all this the women were maintaining a diatribe about how
some bitch was talking shit
or shit talking when you're not there but once you come around
she's all nice and shit
but she jus fuckin pisses me off with her shit
after the first woman paid for her whatever with every last bit of
change
her raggedy ass coin purse could produce
I, like a true gentleman, let the dog carrier of a woman go ahead
of me
so I could see all there is to see see see of this drama unfolding
before me
would you like your receipt? Yes I need to see my EBT balance
while I purchase my convenience I confer with the clerk about
the quality of the drama to which were just privy and the why of it
all
at 30th and Belmont it is more of a neighborhood crowd and less
loitery
welcome to Sandy the BLVD of busted dreams I chimed
as I departed the ladies car lay full frontal in the store's exit and
what a beauty it was

from battered bumper past shattered grill to the hoodless splendor that was the engine
Leading the eye to the license plate laid proudly in the crease where window meets dashboard
I wish I had been more observant as to notice the particular brand of this finely crafted auto
I backed slowly from my space watching the clerk enjoy her tension relieving cigarette
As I carefully passed the ass of that fine blue automobile I noticed it there in the back window
the proud paper plate of a temporary tag displayed high for all to see
A fast splash through the deep gutter puddle along the poorly draining street and I was off
looking forward now wishing I could go back to take more of it in
The not so subtle nuance of the curtain call crawl by the hoodless low riding shock stressed car
filled with low expectations, high drama a Coors tallboy and that sad shivering dog
Is it wrong that the dog is the only one I wanted to save?

Hands

my hands are
tired
dry
puffy
like sausages
stiff
dirty nailed
uncooperative
ready to fight
or punch a wall

my hands have swung hammers
pounded nails
driven stakes
built houses
shined concrete
landscaped
unmanicured
willing to shake
not willing to high five
holding drumsticks
to the grave

to look at one's own hands
is to look at one's own life
all history is there
as you grow older
it is best not to look
on one's hands
unless you
are okay with aging
as the hands
do not lie

these are not
my dad's hands
frightening hands
twisted from use
brown from the sun
blood stained from WW2
these are not my grandfather's hands
severed fingers
left on a factory floor
as he drove his wagon
toward a new life
hand wrapped
in bloody bandages

These are my honest hands
typing
wrinkling
expressing my thoughts
telling my stories
not wishing to punch anything
scars like maps
building relationships
one handshake
at a time

wrong again

It was right there
as my head lay on the wrong pillow
the one that stops my sleep just short of dawn
it was right there
the perfect sentence
the perfect little pearl of an idea
that would propel an entire novel
the grand idea that could very well change society as we know it
no need to write this one down or speak it into my ever-present
digital personal assistant
this is so amazing and clear to me
there is no way I will forget it
Wrong again

SO BE IT
A manifesto?

you want to be a writer?
SO BE IT
sitting pondering my next catchphrase
just to be silly
I thought I would just start saying so be it all the time
and thought better of it
then I broke it down
SO
BE
IT
as cliché as that sounds it is now officially my new mantra, screensaver
written in marker on graph paper and taped to the wall
so simple
so powerful
caps locked
SO BE IT
yesterday a woman at the bakery asked if I was off today
I said actually I am a writer and work from home or coffee shops
as I had just left the coffee shop next-door after an hour of non-writing
and continued to let her know that I am not a very good boss
and should make myself work harder
I did however say
I am a writer
just like that
so it is official then
It is official that I felt comfortable for the first time saying that I am a writer
and if she asked me what I write I probably would not have said crap no one will ever read
Like I always say

SO BE IT
So now I am being it
I am writing
and I will share my writing
so others can say

I have this friend and he is a writer
even if they then say
I have had read some of his stuff and like some of it and he published a book
that will mean that I have not only written but shared that writing with more than
my inner circle

I have the trappings
I got the drinking part down and out of me some time ago
went through the depressed and suicidal part
I own the kind of sweaters a writer should wear
I have many different devices for writing in numerous places
and even more excuses not to use them
now I have the power of being it
sharing it
living it
SO BE IT?
I don't mind if I do

Vegas reflection

my assignment is to write
three hundred crappy words
each day
so I will write three hundred words
for this piece of shit   city
oiled up
like big old titties
this perpetually half empty   glass
of glitz
of crass
of pomp
of
unmitigated circumstance
drinking from
a shrinking corked river
vintage 1935
now more a puddle than a reservoir
headlight tributaries
flow in all directions
past mindless men
with endless erections
topless girls
bottomless drinks
boneless chickens
endless shrinks
in a timeless town
with a vampire's reflection
a sinkhole of
bad intentions
driving fast upon the unfinished
road to recovery
Sun baked and leathery
more naugahyde
Under a morass
of more ass
over indulgence
is the minimum wage of sin

Circles

the hawk circles the neighborhood church
looking for mice feeding quietly on wedding rice
I suppose
causing me to wonder if hawks can only circle
can they not oval
nor triangulate
can fog only roll in and burn off or lift
are there other choices
we are all pigeonholed
I suppose
I wonder if people see me walking the street
and say I am lumbering
what does walking like that have to do with cutting down trees
with ease the hawk surfs the wind currents
banking on a dream of air
fixating on lunch way down there
all hawk-eyed and feather tailed
splitting the the sky like an infinitive
capturing my imagination
infinitely
taking me from the here of the street to the dream of flight
mercurial in its movement
commanding the breeze as well as my fascination
dipping out of sight in the nervous tic of a second
leaving me pondering my day and my place in the world
once again
how often does the hawk go unnoticed
is he always circling me
as I circle the drain

the snake

change
mutate
shed the skin
fan the flames
of the fire within
sin
procreate
ingest the poison
make it your elixir
scream in your own voice
laugh
cry
feel it all fully
get sick with joy
be the victim
the bully
create
explore
dream your life away
your heart will navigate
reminding you how to play

climb till you can no longer breathe
get naked in the rain
accept your true power
fly when you must
act out now or die
a little at a time

page one
on the twenty four hour a day cycle

a sick fascination with celebrity crime
and televised death
a little girl in a small town
royalty and drugs

why does it matter so
occupying your time
and your energy
do you need more blood

is it all for conversation
around the proverbial water cooler
do you have to know it all now
minute by minute
cameras crowding the driveways
trucks with dishes
lining the streets

whose life is worth participation
statistics and battering averages
ballistics and death scene photos
teddy bears lined up along a chain-link fence

that poor little girl
did you hear the latest
I am sure it was the father
I am sure it was that weird anti-social kid dressed in black
I am sure it was the media

enough was too much long ago
but the angry mob craves more
we are all detectives and second guessers
we would have seen it coming
better her than me

Pure Genius

at the hangover breakfast he thanked me
or was it later when we were back on the job
he said you really talked me off a ledge last night or that night
I was ready to quit and you made it all make sense somehow
I really appreciate you being there for me and sharing your
wisdom

the sad reality of this is
after spilling my martini and the bartender giving me another
I don't remember a damn thing I said or did
my heart was in the right place I guess
though my liver was shutting down altogether

I have talked others off the ledge
or so I have been told later
some of these I remember and some I don't
not because I was drunk each time
but because my memory is flawed
the things people say i said to them that really had
such a profound effect on their life
i have no recall of ever saying
nor does it often sound like something I would have said
but I will gladly take the credit

sunset in the alley

on the porch
ambient light
burning through the in between of the houses
the sun is setting

I must head to the back alley to catch a glimpse
I am not disappointed
blue pink, shining white and whimsy
hot asphalt and observations

crack head stumbling along
touching my hand
wishing me well
oh that child of mine she says
as her son asks me for a dollar and fifty cents
I only have a dollar thirty eight

across the alley
open garage door
I inform the neighbor
including crackhead proximity

new next door neighbor filling his dumpster
shakes my hand when he's done
I promise the dogs will get along soon
he has blue stains around his mouth
perhaps frosting
I am surprisingly not threatened by his long hair

the sun has left us now
alone in our houses or lack-thereof
alone with our thoughts
doing private things privately

the sunset brought us together
and sundown leaves us
here and now
which is really all we have

not the cruelest

april is a tease
showing some leg
winking and smiling.
sweet nothing breezes
seem to sing song
"Call me!"
"Call me!"

fickle weather patterns
defy your choice of clothing
bright sun beating
your sweat beading
just before the clouds
and hail

how can I look for work
when the sky is so blue
when the trees begin to bloom
when strong new plants
lift me toward the sun
when it is too wet and cold

april's perfume cannot be resisted
not by monk nor politician
not by teenager nor gravedigger
not even by the loneliest of us
locked in our dim wintery rooms

it's time for a picnic
while the ants are still at rest
and mosquitos do the backstroke.
now before summer's fireball
igniters us and dries up
all that is alive
and we run to our freon cocoons.

galaxy 500

through death valley
i drive a galaxy 500
fast toward sundown
trying to beat the breakdown
spots before my eyes
are white lines
wind at my back
is death's hot exhale

praying for night's fall
skin crawling like a lizard
toward rocky shade
where he can dream
my future.
death dances
with here and now
zen highway blankness

as day turns to dust
and night howls
I hit all four barrels
toss my bottle
to the skeletons
and dream of a gal
in a red rubber ball-gown
as dead friends play dirges
on the cassette deck

awake in a ditch
all sand and bad breath
wishing the valley
would live up to its name.
I just want to combust,
like a magnified ant
ashes to asphalt
spontaneous and free

modern photography

she asked him to delete the photograph
the one he had just taken
she asked this ninety two percent of the time
he politely yet firmly replied
no
she insisted
I don't like the way I look
you seldom do
he countered
I don't want people to see me like this
she demanded
people won't
he countermanded
but I
she interjected
be still
he silenced calmly
I will be the only one to see this photo of you
strongly she reminded him of how she hated to see it
you won't have to
I will be the only one
I think you look ravishing
he bragged
awe
she cooed
he deleted the photo
and they quietly moved forward with life

Impeccable medicine card

I picked a card
or the card picked me
from the cards of medicine
from the native americans
we think
they are animal guides
and they help me
i think
to grow and learn about myself

today the jaguar
hanging from a tree
told me things
like to be
impeccable
a word I know but don't
know that I can be
nor do I know that
I want to be

It is a goal
to be spotless
stainless
flawless
unblemished
I suppose
or maybe it is more
realistic to be
ugly and real

trying to be impeccable
while falling short
has fucked my life
so hard
thinking I was impeccable
made me an ass
made me hard
on myself
obviously

at some point
I should set some goals
I could say could and not should
that is a goal
I was a good goalie when I was young
so I stopped some goals
and that was a success
I digress

the takeaway
is to not want to be
some thing
beyond
what a person can be
but to be the best
u turn
you turn out
to be

Motivationally speaking

It is all about momentum
molding yourself from the clay
of the yesterday
day to day
muck and mire
to rebuild yourself
in your own new image
to your own self inspire
throw some jet fuel
on that fire
until you are consumed by the blaze
of passionate chain reactions
impenetrable from
the nonstop distraction
of an idling mind
for an idling mind is the devil's spaceship
break the gravitational pull
of the impulsive embrace
go deep
go on a lark
just embark
free from guilt
out from under
the omnipresent quilt
of smothering technology
go fetch a stick
to draw a face in the mud
someone may stop and wonder
let em think you've gone mad
let yourself feel that mad feeling
as it could be quite revealing
here here now butterfly
there there now wounded bird
jump on a train just
to see where it ends
aware in each moment
locomotion
momentum
an acted on notion

might be the next big thing
from the ring around the collar
to Sing Sing Sing
head out to the city
or get back to the nature
attend a lecture
on roman nomenclature
expand your horizons along with your parameters
just don't limit yourself to
iambic pentameter

from the void

embracing the darkness
along with the light
falling backwards
two steps forward
is a start
motivation
is it's own reward
with the destination always being right here
procrastination looks beautiful
in the rear view mirror

I am loving the grey backdrop
as it brings focus
to what is close at hand
details are bedeviling
leveling the playing field
sharpening the senses
from the senseless
to a razor brilliance
blinding
with enlightenment
from the void
more jet than coal

seeing the light
is one thing
believing in the dark
is everything
to sing like no one
is alive
to hear like no one
is whispering
to fear
like no one is judging
is to be fearless
seamless is the shadow
endless is the void

choices

you can see in the white light
reflected off wet rocky pavement
galaxies shimmering
if you choose
you can also see misery
if you choose
you could feel empathy
compassion or sympathy
for those sleeping
in flimsy tents
at the bottom of the gully
even if you hold them
in the disdain part
of your brain
even if you call it
a ravine

You can see a rainbow
in the slick oil skin
of the puddle
if you choose
you can also
see the end of the world,
the world
you choose to see
or you can see
beyond the sea
noticing a horizon
in her eyes
right where it used to be
remember it's right there
where it has always been
in the part of your heart
you choose not to see
how it used to be
when you were we
you can choose to be
all that again
your choice

For Elsa

all the time spent
in the pitch black of predawn coldness
not appreciating your patience
not understanding the gift you were giving
we were fake tough together
while both being easily startled
your ears like radars
my mind like thin ice
you showed me the wonders
of everyday life
like a butterfly collection
leaning against a dumpster
like the countless sunrises and sets
full moons like spotlights
new moons like toenail clippings
clouds like a menagerie of ocean life
in and orange and blue sky aquarium
fresh snow quieting the harsh world
as it dusted your coat
making our tracks the first of the day
I can't say where I would be but
I do know I would not be
as likable to me
without your guidance
you saw us through so much
and showed us how diamonds look
dancing on a river
how exciting a splash from
a tossed rock really was
everyone commented on your beauty
no one could see it all
especially not me
not all the time
you helped me meet new friends

while keeping bad people at bay
you were guru and shaman
you were cowriter and protector
your were a reason
when my life had no purpose
you were every cliche
in the best friend kinda way

moments in the sun

they had their
moments
in the sun
and like a
run in the
stocking of
the night sky
they would
not stop
until all the
fun due them
was as exhausted
as they were
finding light
in dark places
made these moments
come alive
and to drive
nowhere
slowly
was a ride of
a lifetime
they headed north
to the back porch
of the island
where waves crashed
and lashed out
at picnics
and would be
beatniks
taking back
the shore
and leaving
them alone
a hike was
a stroll
not a death march
and pleasure
was it's own

reward
on the way
toward
their future
of countless moments in the sun

postcards from the coast

because we are lucky
we are driving along the coast of the Great Pacific Northwest
in a car that is now twelve
yet is still my one and only new car ever
my metal baby
we call her Black Beauty
when we call her
but her gender is ambiguous
It is mid morning
on highway 101
we are dissecting
an Oregon state park
named after the man who gifted us this coast
giant trees surround us
filtering light
filling our eyes
our lungs
I have a strange feeling
of heightened awareness
like something is gonna cross our path
from the right
I am not frightened
just more aware
So I tell her
I have this funny feeling
something is gonna move out in front of us from the right
then just as the last word spills from my mouth
a small bird
jettisons from the trees
on the right
like a shuttlecock
shot from a cannon
yet does not hit nor get hit by
the windshield
but shits
anyhow
on said windshield
and splits our day
into the moment when

that happened
and every other moment
before or after

later
I say things like
I am envisioning large bags of money
up ahead on the right
We play the powerball
but alas and alack
the next day we eat the shittiest lunch
she is in the shiftiest of moods
she is unreadable
yet legible
tension we don't normally feel
knowing better
I eat fish tacos
doused with hot sauce
expelled from a crusty nipple
because I have issues
later I say
that is the kind of lunch that makes
you wish you had bulimia
not that I would write that in a review
late that night
as I try to sleep
my stomach churns
burns
fills with acid
that needs to find
a new home
i am wishing
i did not have this odd
power of precognition

gift of time

I have this gift of time
to catch a squirrel stretch
on a branch
of a tree where there is more
sap today than yesterday
running like icing
from a board nailed
to the bark
how long ago
perhaps it was a step
or a bird feeder mount

I counted ten pines
in a u shape behind our house
I have always seen them
today I used my gift of time
to count them
to notice how they differ
how two next to each other
jut off at the same angle
toward the west just
fifteen feet from the top

I have the gift of time
to notice how green
the moss has become
how much the tree ferns
have come into their own
I walk the yard
in silent meditation
so sure I look
like a madman
starting not to care
I have this gift of time
my gratitude knows no bounds

I have this gift of time
to catalogue all my regrets
relive them

revile them
re-feel them
entirely

to loop the endless loop
of every gaff or blunder
until each new good moment
is cast asunder
missing all the wonder
laid out before me
then this bile filling
systematic filing
begins to bore me
as the splendicity of this day
had begun to ignore me
so I take a deep breath
and glance at the nowness
not knowing how to live in this powerful newness
pretty sure I can just maybe do this
the loop has been broken
the cycle upended
I beg forgiveness from all those I've disappointed
or offended
now with the sun on my face
and the guilt filled quilt lifted
I go back to redeeming
this time I've been gifted

Crow

crow spoke in tongues
on the pole of sizzling power
feathers showing signs of battle
and trips to the other side
he grew enormous
and loud
no one noticed over the
subwoofer/car alarm serenade
crow was soon devoured
by his own shadow
he always is
his shadow devoured the land

looking down upon us with
his eye we call the moon
crow's shadow cried stars
and comets over our souls
no one could see over
the big screen tv safety yard light
shine of our fear of the night

young crow sat powerless on
the swaying branch of youth
feathers all shiny like oil
he screamed for attention
wanting to share all he learned
on his first journey
to the void between thoughts
no one noticed because his
song meant no one any harm
he looked down
first through one eye
then the next
as crow does
seeing no one looking back
he flew off in a spiral
to the sun

early sunday morning at Caffe Vita

She sleeps
I write
watching crows play tag
sharp talons at the ready
as the petit coffee shop
ebbs and flows
with a variety of species
Lattes and smalltalk
Mochas and the weather
Runners in brightly colored shoes
Small dogs
as well as curious toddlers
work patterns into the
painted concrete floor

It's Sunday
and no-one looks dressed for church
It's more like we all detached ourselves
from our beds
smelled the fresh coffee
like so much blood in the water
and started circling

the espresso grinder screams
like a small child just told they can't
have a new toy
the click click of the doser is
a woodpecker to me
followed by the Godzilla-like cry
of the of the steam wand
kissing milk

the wind moves branches
like a depressed woman
looking endlessly though racks
of discounted dresses
never choosing one
always knowing nothing
would look good on her anyway

a couple rolls up to the curb
early sunday morning at Caffe Vita continued

in a shiny black Pathfinder
she unfolds herself from the passenger side
my side
Jeans cuffed halfway up her calf
in a post rockabilly Pulp Fiction kind of way
he rounds the car
looking all Daddy's money
ray bans protecting his eyes
from the slate grey sky
they each seem to
be lacking the necessary
amount of self loathing
required to be a real human being
I think

I sit in judgement
like a time lapse camera
over here in the corner
life is perfect

Living out loud

It is the late night now
where I am
thankful for the quiet
the heat
the day
warmth and walls
hearth and heartbeat
grapes and fermentation
the clothes on me
the earthy taste of the magical tea
that brings me to this brink of now

I am grateful to find me here in a way I have never known
so fully in this seemingly non-momentous moment
momentously happy to simply be
and also to know no one is videoing me
or at least I think they are not
I mean the microwave is right over there
I sit by an uncurtained window
in an uncertain world

all roads lead to me being thankful my life does not live
In too many places on the internet
my embarrassments are
my embarrassments
to be re-lived internally mentally
ad nauseam
by me and
anyone
I can only guess
it would be egotistical of me to think anyone else remembered any
of me
even the worst moments I replay eternally
what I mean is
is anyone as mean to me as I
is anyone
as mean to anyone as I
am to me

if I could get there from here perhaps I would think that people who have had their lives loaded up the down staircase of the tubeless tube to become the latest nincompoop or rube are no worse off
than one living in a private viewing room

so much buckshot

my mind scatters like so much bird seed on the cold winter ground
My thoughts are however less useful
no nourishment
an unfocused lens
so much buckshot
fired at clouds
a colorblind butterfly
pollinating Veterans Day poppies

the cold morning unfolds
hipsters recoil
skinny jeans
cling to skinny legs
pushing fixie pedals
love their determination

the medical marihuana store
opens early
even on sunday
wake and bake
the world evolves
in each minute

in between

It's 3:13 AM or so
and the cats are on me like hyenas
on fresh kill
the big guy pinning my shoulder
marking my jawline
the little one tucking in behind my knees
to jackknife my legs
they move like long time tag team wrestling partners
I'm so thirsty yet I don't want to disturb them
so aware that the life preserver of sleep
drifted toward the pitch black horizon ten minutes ago
so not wanting to wake her
so not wanting to lose my dreamy genius

I am not cool enough to be an insomniac
just like we were not rich enough to have allergies as kids
I am just old enough to need a bathroom break
around this time
or I am being healthier by drinking enough water
to wake even a younger me
around this time
this time when a younger me would have been passing out
after the show
ears still ringing a bit
beer already turning to sour morning breath behind my dopey
curled smile
close curtain
cue the dream cycle
prepare hangover

the house is glossy and still ship shape from her return
the order eases my mind
the shiny countertop creates puddles of digital clock mockery
of my sleeplessness
as the cliche train whistle blows though no one would believe me
heading to parts well mapped
I think now that I did not sleep so much as I napped
as I splash cold water on my eyelids
to bring me from the in-between

to the thought hunter gatherer typist mode
we've lost a lot of good words to this state of mind
and dammit I am not about to lose any more

I fret over every sound even the dogs tap dancing claws on the floorboards

So glad now that I oiled the hinges
so glad now that I live in an age of soft computer keyboards
and not woodpecker typewriters with their bells and crumpled paper edits
She wakes in spite of my church mouse morphing
I increase my stealth
she returns to bed without crossing the threshold
She needs her sleep
not for beauty
but to wash away the sins of her unending workload
to slay the dragons of travel and the low slung arrows of petty tyrants
emailing edicts and ultimatums at all times of day and now
Sleepless slitherers hissing and moaning in an effort to make their jobs seem necessary
Bringing meaning to the meaningless

just before I awoke
I sat next to a man at the end of a u-shaped bar facing west
he was to my right trying to win the cracker jack game so tiny in his hands
all angles were attempted tongue slung over his lip like Sinatra's jacket
over the shoulder of his tailored shirt
the dude Exuding so much frustration upon not winning this un-winnable game
then my dream narrator spoke frankly in my mind's ear saying
and this guy is the head of maintenance at the country's largest nuclear plant?
I think I am glad I awoke before that dream played out
let's go see what dreams the couch will conjure
she needs her sleep
and so do I

tenth and yamhill

sitting pleasantly behind glass here at the corner of tenth and Yamhill
always wondering if there used to a yam farm around here back in the day
I will leave that a mystery for now
watching all the beautiful people walk by
beautifully dressed
meticulously coiffed
gorgeously touched in the head
as they used to say
before they knew better

this corner is a bonanza, a mother-load
a veritable smorgasbord of humanity
displaying varying degrees of connectivity to the physical world around them
or to the various parallel realities available to those on the correct wavelength
not all antennae pick up all channels
not all vagrants are, by design, vandals
tourists from the downtown hotels abound
surrounded by the bountiful mixed up menagerie of people who live in the what used to be
shouting their poetic histories into the sea of anonymity
with a profound proclivity

shriek

the shrill shriek of the the stellar jay wakes me from
the sleepwalking part of my morning meditation causing
me to seek out this cobalt blue fighter jet of a bird
he simplifies this by screeching through his ascent
to perch on the telephone pole that holds no telephone lines
anymore but perhaps is a totem to the home telephone of the past
the bird makes no call from up there but does his interpretive dance instead
ducking like a prize fighter trying to avoid a repeated jab
I realize he could be a she as maybe the blue is not so blue
and the size is lacking
I like to extrapolate based on my sub base knowledge of ornithology
at this point the robin struts by looking like an usher at a fancy theatre
or prize fight arena
the scrub jay grows weary of his lack of an audience and zip-lines across the street
silently
I have to get out on the porch more often if all this action is happening
I think
I can also use these outdoor visitations to track the progress of the tree moss
and find new ways to describe precipitation and the subtle differences of grey in the sky
while I wonder if the neighbors are also pondering the reason for my existence

bring in the clowns

each day starts
with such promise
it's all sunshine
coffee
big plans
trumpeting elephants
barker's call
hungover clowns
rumbling by
in a tiny car
with big shoes
to fill
the hearts of both
young and old
with joy

coffee wears off
the sun gets oppressively hot
ambition fades
you spin in circles
all nerves
and fear
as the taste of failure
settles in

elephants are chained to poles
the barker is shouting at his wife
the clowns are on a drunken rampage
step
right
up
step
right
up

guns and blood

he makes her laugh,
she forgives him
for his lack of
motivation

sometimes she laughs
but is uncomfortable
at the same time,
she is scared

he says things that
are very off the wall,
he spends a lot of
time alone

he needs her
more than she knows,
she is his tether
to the world

he scares himself
more than anyone imagines,
his thoughts go out to others
through elaborate filters

At 2:34 am he shakes
and sometimes cries,
contemplating
his own demise,

he is a hero
to her
he was happy once
he is sure of it,

thank god he hates
guns and Blood

evolution

change
everything
put yourself
in shock
go into
hock
quit
everything
you thought
you had to
finish
disappear
but
don't diminish
find yourself
by letting
yourself
get lost
wander
through
someplace
scary and
new
expect nothing
cherish that
nothing
more than
all the
somethings
that used to
move you,
you're fired
you're dead
you are alone
nobody loves you
anymore than you
love yourself

spontaneous pop song

her torment was obvious
the dead falling leaves make me sad
she screamed as they drove her away
i just ate at myself up from inside

her tears were a river of fear
my thoughts were all of myself
her pain could be felt by all
i felt nothing except for the wind

she cried why why why must i go
i'm better now
i just got upset
why do you push me away
when i flew all this way on the plane

she's just a memory now
a story i'll tell to my friends
her illness will be fixed by some pills
or she'll die and i'll never know

and she cried
why why why can't i stay
I'm better now i just wanna
why can't i come inside
and tell them about all this love

less

It takes less and less
to make myself all
scary these days
just a scrunch of the brow
and presto
I am a frightening man
all werewolf and such

It takes less and less
sadness to make me
frightening these days
just one poem and
off they go
down the stairs
right to
"oh my god
I thought I knew him"

a wing and a prayer

spring reveals itself
one morsel at a time
a crocus here
a bright green bud becoming a leaf there
the branch itself on the Japanese maple
morphing like a chameleon
to reveal a new virescent skin
to those who make time to notice
to those of us who are lucky
or bored
or useless otherwise
with nothing to contribute to society
nothing that can be monetized extracted exploited or
reconnoitered

the birds' songs shift in tone and exuberance
just as their dance pivots toward mating
anticipating the warm winds to follow
swallows returning for cappuccino
along with various and sundry pastries
making a nest then lying in it
built of g-strings and pasties
fishnets fished from the dumpsters
behind club swish swish swish
where fishers of men become hunters
and the spoon falls in love with the dish

518 AM In Tempe

a house detective-like knock on the hotel door
crack crack crack crack crack
the loud concrete hotel room bounces the sound
like a pinball to my bumper slumber head
I confusedly dress forgetting about the peephole
by the time I am at the door
they are not
why did I feel so obliged to answer?
why did I waste my shut eye?
when do I ever call sleep shut eye?

back in bed I drift in and out
I have been up half the night
waist deep in the rooftop pool
ushering sleepy jets to rest
upon the all too nearby quilted tarmac
one filterless Chesterfield in each hand
lungs hurting from keeping them lit
somehow feeling duty bound
to bring those giants safely to the ground
lives are at stake I keep mumbling
lives are at stake
I wave my hands to the left slowly
the pilot proudly salutes

back under the covers
treading sleepy water
I invent a friend
Vladimir the cagey bee
aka the red hornet
aka I must be very tired to find this so amusing
the room is dark
the air is stagnant
the bed is firm and friendly
I am lucky
I can walk away
into the desert's waiting arms
wondering if scorpions scream
before they strike

heard

I am not trending
nor do I ever intend to be
right now
my mind is bending
like a spoon
business end ending
back toward the shaft
that is my spine
curved like an S
hurting my mind
pain unending
anger trending
tending to make me a dick
because when I am sick
or hurting painfully
I become disdainfully repugnant
spending my time knitting
by this I mean nitpicking
needling those who sew my life together
those who tether me through bad weather
as they weather my stormy Mondays
through all the unending days
ending in why me
what did I do to deserve this
I am not giving it up
I am not taking the piss
I am shooting straight from the hip
the pain is shooting
straight through my
hypocrisy
toward the woman who puts up with
the bullshit that is me
even though her pain is far beyond
the sea that I can see
reaching depths
twenty thousand leagues beneath
the surface tension I could wrap my arms around, fathom or mention
then she texts
saying simply

I love you
with the subtext
I know you are hurting
subsubtext:
you are kinda being a dick

The Virgin Berth

I just passed my bedtime
waiting to find my prime time
with one foot in the breadline
marching to the beat of
a million bakers
tired of shakers
who just don't move me baby
so I wanna get real gone for a change
looking for a fissure in men
I am fishing in the shallow waters
within the protective reef
of my comfortable belief
eco systems
free from floods
both biblical
and familial
Jesus Christ begging for some change
who amongst us will wash his feet?
I am living high on the hog
fighting for scraps with the junkyard dogs
scratching mythical itches
biting anything that twitches
labeling anything I don't understand
as science or witches
traveling across the rails
in a virgin berth
the world passing by like a dream
believing it all
or nothing at all
while picking ripe cherries
from Eden's garden of trees
just outside the wall
that's where you'll find me
spitting seeds at any who will dodge them
hoping they might slip upon
the love they hide deep
for those of us creeping in the night

train of skitchin thoughts

okay
so I am superstitious
a black cat just sat on my keyboard
well
maybe I am not superstitious
just a creature of habit
because the beginning of
Out Of This World by John Coltrane
has begun so many things I have written
so many things I like that I have written
so much so
I feel I must keep this song at the starting line
of any writing playlist
not that I need music to write
this song is just the catalyst
the musical stimulus package
of my mind's pen
the chaotic zen
of the typecast writer
the *nom de plume*
I have become
too many writing options
and too much time
combined with a certain comfort level
makes me a dullard
with a never ending blank slate
as well as a fist full of excuses
with a list full of unfulfilled ideas
piling up in the landfill
of thoughts unspilled
never getting my own gist
another pint so I'll be too pissed
to babble on
to Babylon
and beyond
I set sail
yet most days
get derailed
from the tracks of achievement

into the shiny objectifying lake
of drowned sorrows
if you get to better tomorrows
you've gone too far
yet not enough
to call your own bluff
so you will have to read the cliff
notes from a dirty old pen
digitally compressed
from the repressed
recesses of a mind
terribly wasted
on ditch-weed, nerves
and flavors untasted
you can't get here from there
because the starting line
keeps shifting like
a nobody's fault but mine
line of questioning
of tectonic suggestioning
smelling of magic potions
pimp oils, sundries and notions
evoking emotions
bought or sold
on the black market boardwalk
the clicketty clack
transcontinental spike
of adrenalin born of
peaks and valleys
dirges and rallies
boulevards and alleys
all shiny with
the oil stains of progress
yet i digress
back to the stress fracturous
times when push came to
shovel
and shovels sold at a premium
blizzards so epic
are much more fun
when you dream of them
bald tires on sheets of ice

bring back the futility
of an angel dusted youth
wasted on the young
while skitchin a ride
on the bumper
of an oldsmobile
one with the truth
danger is fun

Fight

just after work
waiting for the light at 22nd
I saw two men start to fight
allowing time to lose loose clothing
then right to it
both showed good form
almost Marquis of Queensbury
I was sad when my light turned green
so I slowed to a stop as I turned the corner
then came to my senses as I am not the type
to sponsor senseless violence
so I drove off
only pausing for a split
to ponder a rounding of the block

now I think
who was I to judge if this was senseless?

Why the fight?
I still wonder
Their skin was not like-colored
yet not far off
they looked differently aged
they looked equally drugged
equally determined
I thought less of myself for wanting to watch
now I feel lame for not knowing who won
if they were arrested or stopped
if they drew a crowd
if they drew blood
if they drew weapons

I should not be surprised by my lack of surprise
when I saw this brawl
I work in a tempestuous part of town
where many people live their lives on the sidewalk
so close to the curb
the jetsam assembling shelters from flotsam

booting up and drinking down
while newcomers move into overpriced nooks
to be close to it all
the millennial Jetset assembling Swedish furniture
swilling designer drugs and trendy beer

I feel so much anger
every day
and can't make sense
of that anger
we all make choices
I think
we all face hardship
or not
many of the street dwellers here seem
to be sidewalk sailing
on a nonstop party yacht
or dingy I guess
while we work around them
and their mess

I know there are many stories
of the how and why they are here
I also know some of these people
are partying hard
while using my backyard
as their bathroom and dumpster
and I know there has to be a better
way and where for them to live
perhaps people can pay
to watch the fights
or we can all just
be honest

snow tires

it's beyond hot
July won't release its grip
her studded snow tires rip
into the close-to-melting pavement
the noise takes her back
as it often does
as noises often do
to late last November
he was installing the tires
after months of prodding
how hard should this be for a mechanic?
the cobbler's kids have no shoes
she thought
as the air wrench whinnied and hammered
while empty beer cans whistled toward the recycling bin
toward her
this one last time

she is headed now
toward the mountains
toward home
or the house that once was all that
to the kids who are constant reminders
of the love that once was
all that
and the setting sun
setting on him
on the other side of these mountains
blinds her
reminds her
of the day he took the love and ran
toward that setting sun
unsettling one and all
here in the land that he forgot
that, at least, is her abbreviated,
while often inebriated,
story

the aforementioned used steel belted radials

spun onto her fifteen year old honda accord
now sing mezzo-soprano
as the auto achieves highway speed
with the percussion section
of loose body panels and soda cans
keeping an uneven time
the pebble in the last remaining hubcap
now conducted to silence by centrifugal force
she reaches out lightning fast
to catch Skyler's hand drawn valentines-day card
as it catches air
arching toward the leaky sunroof
if there were Olympic honors for this action
she would be the winningest
gold medalists
of all time

She holds the heart shaped card
against the heart shaped tattoo
just above her
still shapely
left breast
a tear drops
tracing her high cheek bone
reflecting the bright rays
like a crystal pendant
hung from the mirror
of a new-age driver

all this brings her back to
her latest mantra
the one that resonates
like no other
the one that helps keep
her sadness at bay
so she begins to chant
go fuck yourself
go fuck yourself
go mother fucking fuck yourself
for the next ten miles or so
as dusk becomes evening
sadness becomes strength

Let Us Prey

I walk out to the back yard
heading to the downstairs
the down there
to change the locks
to keep our
wayward contractor
out of our here

just outside the door
I see a flutter of wings
up to the peach tree
big spotted thing
bigger than anything
winged
in our yard
i have ever seen

we exchange glances
sideways and otherwise
calm and excited
I run for my wife
a hawk in our yard!
she leaves her girly network bliss
to take a gander
at the goose
that is this

the hawk performs an awkward dance
from fence to fence
weak branch to flimsy branch
all the time keeping us in check
making us believe he is a refuge
from the nearby zoo
from an aviary
secretly we hoped
he was the grim reaper of squirrels

seeing a stealthy bird
of prey

wagging its tail feathers
over our fence
here in the city
is obtuse at best
unnerving yet calming
at worst
suddenly our hawkish friend
shoots toward the top of the peach tree
reaches it with a smack
and heads toward the sunset
best as I can tell

my hawk eyed wife
who sees animals when no one else can
quickly points to the spotty chested bird
now high in a neighbor's tree
a small bird pinned beneath it's talons
slowly being disemboweled
one of those we have fed and watched
all summer
the hawk
plucking away

life transferred from prey
to predator

So unsettling to watch
with me so unwilling to look away
like a nature film
spinning through the projector
of our back yard
archived in our memories
under
shrill death cry of a songbird

Storm's a comin

I walk our street looking like the grim reaper
pulling down my lid
against the afternoon wind
there is no eye in team
but there is one in
hurricane i think
or an eye in typhoon
If that's what you wanna call it

the air smells dangerous
the trees are taking the fifth
though they are dropping leaves
and pieces of branches
like cluster bombs

the sky glows green here
black to the north
blue to the west
the air is soft
as always
leaves spin in
tiny funnel clouds

I expect to see an old man
leaning over a corral like fence
chewing on a straw and saying
storm's a comin
worst one in forty some odd years they say
better hunker down

I nod my head to oncoming cars as if to say
howdy neighbor
our streets are so tiny
without sidewalks
most folks who drive them live around here
so I am not out of line
if I am
I could not care less
a nod is a good as a wink

to a blind horse

the storm turns out to be
like so many things
just some cable channel hype
getting folks all riled up
worrying for no good reason
about something out of their control
like an election cycle
spinning
into the apocalypse

nashville gloom

last night in room 615
I dreamt of a man with tiny hands
trying to live in a big manhandled world
I was getting ski lessons
strapping cucumbers to my feet
in a lush green back yard.
I awoke to the humid southern air
licking my face like a St Bernard
then wrapping me in a fat soft palm
as i left the hotel

grey skies provide a moody backdrop
for the dirty old buildings
as well as the shiny new
monuments to fast wealth
soon I will jump into the honky tonk
lined tourist trap
wishing I was wearing boots
instead of sandals
wishing i was drunk
slightly scandalous

the trap is called because of rain
so I walk past statues of dead southerners
toward the market of farmers
with southern food holding court nearby
all fried chicken with three sides
matching cuffs and collards
cafeteria style

I should feel thin here
but I am guilty
none the less
sucking in my gut
till my back hurts
today I daydreamed of a thin man
living in a fat mans shirt
today I walked a tight rope

drawing a fine line
in the swamp
of my willpower

now
blurry in the hotel atrium
lost in my own electronic world
John Coltrane
fueling my creative fire
I burn zeros and ones till the
cows turn to BBQ
or till the unintelligible maid
finishes with our room
so sure she is fantasizing
about me now
the south will writhe again

corn husks and crickets

corn husks and crickets
summer is right now
it is tonight
with a perfect temperature
for sleeping
without fall creeping
around all Sancho
stealing our summer brides
It is open screened windows and doors
open minds
all thinking
 planning
running wild in the streets
all sweet flower smells
backyard barbecue
all right now
back then
when our skin
was still hot
from a hard days work
when we were darker
in the shower
than out on the street
when money and a suntan
was all that we had
and less than we needed
when girls were scarce like diamonds
and drugs ran like scalded dogs
toward our wallets
when life was worth living
and living was worth a good god damn
man that first dip
toward the stumble
then the trip

was so
toe in the water
fun
all crumble
laugh a minute rumble
never now trade it for
a fumble
no regrets
no epithets
no tumbles
now
in the nightcap
tumbler
top shelf whisky
I do not grumble
upper crust always
always a layer or
two above my skin
no trade in
no take back
no fake
no more
than this
peach fuzz skin
taking in
that summer wind

Connect with Me

Visit me at

www.perhimself.com

or

http://www.Twitter.com/PerHimself

About Pér

Pér Himself has lived a multitude of lives, worked a multitude of jobs, and played in countless punk, rockabilly, and hard-to-classify bands. From digging ditches to singing telegrams, Pér has done it all while writing with the passionate heart that beats in all great American poets. Pér observes life from unique angles, bringing a syncopated view of the world around and within to readers in a relatable and often humorous way. Pér finds it funny anyway.

From Pér Himself About Pér Himself

In the fifth grade I wrote "I HATE HATE HATE MYSELF!" in the top margin of a school paper on which I received a bad grade I knew then that I had to be a writer.That is only half true. I did write that, fully unaware that the paper had to be turned back into the teacher.. I did not know then that I had to be a writer but I did learn that I had to be a bit more discreet about my self-loathing.

That was then.

Much of my life has not really been lived fully in the moment because I've been mostly thinking about how I am going to write about the moment in a way that will invite someone who was not there to share the moment, to help someone who was there relive the moment, or both. This is a good thing. Once I heard someone laugh or saw them tear up over something I had written I felt a connection like none I had ever known. I hope my writing will connect us in some meaningful way.

If creativity exists it finds its way to the light. One might pour themselves into their work or into their family or just pour themselves another drink until they become an expert at something even if that expertise is in avoiding doing what they love because they are afraid. A love of language whether written spoken or sung has woven it's way into everything I have done as a JOB whether that was rewriting an entire singing telegram routine on the fly, inserting inside jokes into drink menu descriptions or talking a fellow employee off the cliff. The best feeling of all was surprising a guest who was having a rough day by making them smile, remembering their story or giving them a free pancake (God bless Snooze An AM Eatery!).

www.ingramcontent.com/pod-product-compliance
Lightning Source LLC
Chambersburg PA
CBHW031558040426
42452CB00006B/341